TAKE A BITE
OUT OF JESUS

Dear Angie

Live Forever!

Enjoy Rod Hempl

Take a Bite
Out of Jesus
Healing Bread That Strengthens Us

Rodney Alan Hempel

ELM HILL

A Division of
HarperCollins Christian Publishing

www.elmhillbooks.com

Take a Bite Out of Jesus

Healing Bread That Strengthens Us

Published in Nashville, Tennessee, by Elm Hill, an imprint of Thomas Nelson. Elm Hill and Thomas Nelson are registered trademarks of HarperCollins Christian Publishing, Inc.

Elm Hill titles may be purchased in bulk for educational, business, fund-raising, or sales promotional use. For information, please e-mail SpecialMarkets@ThomasNelson.com.

Library of Congress Cataloging-in-Publication Data

Library of Congress Control Number: 2019912386

ISBN 978-1-400328536 (Paperback)
ISBN 978-1-400328543 (Hardbound)
ISBN 978-1-400328550 (eBook)

CONTENTS

ACKNOWLEDGMENTS

Looking back, it seems that my personal witness is only possible because of the Christian foundation that has been built in me through the discipleship of others who shared their love of Jesus. Thanks to retired Pastor Richard Bradford and Pastor Tedd Manning of the Ellicott City Assembly of God. My fellow church members who participated with me in twenty-five years of Bible study. Also, I give special thanks to my beloved wife, Rachelle, who is blessed with the gifts of having integrity, patience, faithfulness, and being my lifelong helpmate. Thanks be to the Lord Almighty for their fellowship. And finally, to my parents, August and Dorothy Hempel, for their love and dedication shown to every family member.

CHAPTER 1

BE AWARE OF YOUR
ENVIRONMENT

You Can Get Thorns

My **father,** named August, who recently passed, used to say these words daily to me as a young boy, "Be aware of your environment!" I took his message to mean that I needed to become a more careful observer of events and look for the deeper meaning of things. So, I have tried to look deeper and form a wiser understanding of many things, and deeper into the meaning and motives of others. By the way, my pop had quite a few snappy lines like "How fast do you think that you think?"

These sayings encouraged me to act patiently, to always be learning, and to not be impulsive in situations that were over my head. By taking careful steps, a person can become an explorer of complicated ideas. Let's hope that I will still follow his advice. With humility, I want to share a short story of some recent life-changing events that helped me find purpose and spiritual encouragement when circumstances became overwhelming for me. All of us will encounter heartbreaking health, career, financial, family, or relationship "thorns" on our life journey. I have had to live through several of these unpleasant episodes. Through these difficulties, my spiritual insight matured and a stronger faith formed in my witness of the Lord Jesus.

There is a fundamental human desire to walk our purposeful lives—to have a life of meaning that satisfies. As we journey through our days, many folks seek to find self-worth in pursuing their specially given purpose—to leave their personal mark of making a better world for others, to have a personal significance—a life that rocks their world.

Some examples might be striving to offer an outstanding business service or product; perhaps building a winning sports team; or becoming involved in social causes, seeking leadership to guide others, researching unknown mysteries, or simply shooting the lowest golf score may satisfy.

In their purposeful pursuits, many people also find spiritual contentment with having found a deeper purpose in serving the Lord Almighty. A few years ago, the best-selling book, *The Purpose Driven Life*,[1] was written by Christian pastor Rick Warren. The book continues to be a wonderful encouragement to those who become fulfilled with a sense of significance in serving our Lord Jesus. Great joy and peace usually accompany those in Christ, even during hardships.

For those without a faith-based purpose, they also find purpose in pursuing their given talents using their curiosity and dedication in their chosen occupation—being of public service in their community, or just serving the needs of families and loved

---

[1] Rick Warren, *The Purpose Driven Life* (Grand Rapids: Zondervan, 2002)

ones. Without this sense of fulfilling a purpose, perhaps our auto-biographies would simply be titled "What For?" Another of my father's sayings.

Then there is the entire Book of Ecclesiastes written by King Solomon, who tries to impart his wisdom to fulfilling one's pursuit of purpose.

From Ecclesiastes 3:22:

> "So I saw that there is nothing better for a person than to enjoy their work, because that is their lot. For who can bring them to see what will happen after them?"

And from Ecclesiastes 12:12–14:

> "Of making many books there is no end, and much study wearies the body. Now all has been heard; here is the conclusion of the matter: Fear God and keep his com-mandments, for this is the duty of all mankind. For God will bring every deed into judgment, including every hid-den thing, whether it is good or evil."

As we share great joy in blessed times, we also share great sor-rows in comforting one another during challenging times. Being aware of our environment, we discover that, as time and circum-stances pass, certain limits have indeed been placed on our ability to serve others and pursue purposeful lives to the extent we were once capable. The pursuit of a purpose driven life gets increasingly limited with age. Age limitations are not of our choosing. They arise and have a power of their own and we all acknowledge and yield to them. They grow to be greater than us, thereby causing us to alter the path of our purpose driven lives.

Eventually, everyone has life challenges that cause us to

struggle. Indeed, even the apostle Paul had a "thorn" placed in his productive life while in service to the Lord Almighty. The sovereign Lord, for his good and pleasing purpose, desired to shape Paul's path. He granted permission to Satan's messengers to humble Paul.

Being humbled is a necessary part of a spiritual learning curve which is intended to better align us with the Lord Almighty's will. I will call this learning curve "Life becomes a progressive realization."

What once was hidden suddenly gets revealed. We all share this as a common experience; boundaries are being laid before us all. We would be wise to reflect upon the limitations that God *allows to* happen to us. The Lord Almighty is sovereign and is directing our path.

Paul shares with us his experience with his acquired limitations in 2 Corinthians 12:7–9. Note that Paul is resigned that the Lord is sovereign and resolute in these matters. In fact, Paul further boasts upon his struggles in 2 Corinthians 11:23–33. Here is Paul's take on the matter of his life limiting boundaries.

From 2 Corinthians 12:7–9:

> "Therefore, in order to keep me from becoming conceited, I was given a thorn in my flesh, a messenger of Satan, to torment me. Three times I pleaded with the Lord to take it away from me. But he said to me, 'My grace is sufficient... for my power is made perfect in weakness.'"

Note that the one given limited permission to place a thorn in Paul's side is a messenger of Satan.

The Book of Job also describes a similar experience that is painful to read. Satan, after searching the world, asks permission from the Lord Almighty to sift Job. Job then gets a boatload of thorns and desires the Lord to explain why he deserves such

4

torment. Job was a righteous man who needed a godly explanation for why there are so many torments. Job eventually had his one-on-one discussion with the Lord Almighty, after which he comes to the viewpoint that the Lord Almighty is just, possesses all wisdom, *is loving,* and is sovereign.

As my pop said, "Be aware of your environment." Indeed, the Lord Almighty is sovereign. All things work to his pleasant and pleasing will. The "thorns" teach us humility; indeed, the Lord Almighty is sovereign and strong in our weakness. Whereas, the present world teaches us to never cease to compete for our lot in life. And there is much approval, recognition, and award given when we are temporarily powerful and victorious. But as we age, this ability to compete fails in all of us. Seeking power that lasts is wise.

CHAPTER 2

WE ALL WILL NEED
A NEW BODY

Jesus Offers His to Us

So, there will be thorns along our journey. Expect them. I would like to speak personally about a pair of them that were recently permitted to manifest themselves in my path. Surprisingly, I was able to ignore them for many years before realizing that these "thorns" were surely bringing me to a full stop.

Amazingly, this was the fourth time that "thorns" had fully stopped many of my purposeful activities. And every one of my "thorns" eventually became the number one priority to navigate around. A full stop of all other purposeful plans was needed to learn how to manage these "thorns" before resuming my life activities.

Previously, two older "thorns" had affected my health and the third ended my business career. I'll briefly speak more about these times in Chapter 3.

These more recent "thorns" can be simply described as having both of my knees fail with aging. It became so painful to walk that they brought everything to a full stop. There was little enjoyment in pursuing any physical activity. Walking a hundred yards was problematic.

Over a few years, both knees had developed such significant osteoarthritic damage that there was no longer any medial meniscus remaining. This, in turn, caused the femur to severely misalign with the hip socket. The pain became so great that I couldn't walk a hundred yards without resting.

The prognosis was that I needed to undergo two separate total knee replacement surgeries. No stem cell cure or slick oil would work for my condition.

This time, I would be humbled again by my failing body. And this time, I was given the task by the Lord to share my new spiritual understanding with like-minded servants of our Father in heaven. The Lord wanted to provide a modern-day witness to convey his much needed solution to people's health problems.

Listen to the perspective of Jesus about our desperate human condition.

From John 6:32–40 (emphasis added):

> "Jesus said to them, 'Very truly I tell you, it is not Moses who has given you the bread from heaven, but it is my Father who gives you the true bread from heaven. For the bread of God is the bread that comes down from heaven and gives life to the world.' 'Sir,' they said, 'always give us this bread.' Then Jesus declared, 'I am the bread of life. Whoever comes to me will never go hungry, and whoever believes in me will never be thirsty. But as I told you, you have seen me and still you do not believe. All those the

Father gives me will come to me, and…I will never drive away. For I have come down from heaven not to do my will but to do the will of him who sent me. And this is the will of him who sent me, that I shall lose none of those he has given me, **_but raise them up at the last day._** For my Father's will is that everyone who looks to the Son and believes in him shall have eternal life, and **_I will raise them up at the last day._**"

Jesus was immediately challenged and further pressed for the meaning of him being the bread that comes down from heaven. Again, he responds.

From John 6:48–65 (emphasis added):

"'I am the bread of life. Your ancestors ate the manna in the wilderness, yet they died. But here is the bread that comes down from heaven, which anyone may eat and not die. I am the living bread that came down from heaven. Whoever eats this bread will live forever. This bread is my flesh, which I will give for the life of the world.'

Then the Jews began to argue sharply among themselves, 'How can this man give us his flesh to eat?'

Jesus said to them, 'Very truly I tell you, unless you eat the flesh of the Son of Man and drink his blood, you have no life in you. Whoever eats my flesh and drinks my blood has eternal life, and **_I will raise them up at the last day._** For my flesh is real food and my blood is real drink. Whoever eats my flesh and drinks my blood remains in me, and I in them. Just as the living Father sent me and I live because of the Father, so the one who feeds on me will live because of me. This is the bread that came down from heaven. Your ancestors ate manna and died, but whoever feeds on this bread will live forever.' He said this while teaching in the synagogue in Capernaum.

On hearing it, many of his disciples said, 'This is a hard teaching. Who can accept it?'

Aware that his disciples were grumbling about this, Jesus said to them, 'Does this offend you? Then what if you see the Son of Man ascend to where he was before! The Spirit gives life; the flesh counts for nothing. The words I have spoken to you—they are full of the Spirit and life. Yet there are some of you who do not believe.' For Jesus had known from the beginning which of them did not believe and who would betray him. He went on to say, 'This is why I told you that no one can come to me unless the Father has enabled them.'"

And finally, from John 6:66–69:

"From this time many of his disciples turned back and no longer followed him. 'You do not want to leave too, do you?' Jesus asked the Twelve.

Simon Peter answered him, 'Lord, to whom shall we go? You have the words of eternal life. We have come to believe and to know that you are the Holy One of God.'"

Upon first hearing Jesus in this passage, I first thought of taking Communion. We usually think of Jesus's broken body sacrificed for our sins as we partake and then crunch up that unleavened bread. But now, I'm thinking that Jesus is also offering us to take a bite of not only his broken, sacrificed body but also the resurrected body—the eternal body of Jesus! Yes! I, too, want an eternal, powerful, full of life body. I'm pretty tired of repairing this one. And so, here, Jesus is offering his! Instructing me to also partake in all conditions of *his body*! Not only his broken flesh *but also* his perfect resurrected body! He is offering an eternal life in a new body! God's plan is that we completely share the same experience as Jesus—from fully broken to raised up body! His power is indeed perfected in my weakness!

So yes! I will take a big bite of Jesus! We all need to! Yes, I want a big bite! I need a big bite! I need a resurrected body like Jesus. This one is weak and getting weaker. But I guess that I'll have to wait until that last day to get the promised new body. I'll just have to struggle on with the one given to me for a bit more. *If it's God's* will to heal, my two knees can be repaired and maybe work as good as the originals!

The next chapter will tell more about some of my life history in this failing body. I certainly do need a new body. Indeed, eventually, we will all pass this same way. Every one of us! We share a common fate. We all need resurrected bodies! Please don't walk away like those other disciples did. Stay like the Twelve did.

CHAPTER 3

SOMEONE NEEDS TO
BE MY GUIDE

The Way Forward

There is much joy in celebrating all the Lord's blessings bestowed upon our lives. I was having so much fun sharing in the joy of the Lord, that I was truly blindsided and unprepared for the new limit the Lord had permitted to be placed in my aging life path. I'm so thankful for a wonderful believing family, great lifelong friends, diligent parents, supportive siblings, fellow believers, a sound mind, and on and on.

Being sifted and tested by the Lord Almighty after all the blessings that have been given to me was a surprise! It totally caught me off guard thinking his grace was all blessings; difficult times were in my past, foolishly just enjoying the moment.

With another go around on "thorn management," I decided to reflect upon those previously difficult times. So as to learn from my past, here are the three previous times when serious life-changing limits were permitted to be placed upon me. I'll call these times "when you come to the end of yourself." A new path must be taken. Truly a moment for repentance.

The first was when I was diagnosed with diabetes at age forty. Diabetes is a lifelong eroding disease that attacks every part of one's body. The actual blood sugar level in a diabetic person needs to be monitored four times a day. Finger sticks, insulin pens, doctor's quarterly checkups, A1C blood tests, etc., etc. Failure to control blood sugar can lead to major health complications. Thank you, Dr. Hagen for twenty-five years of supervising care.

Then the second limitation came on Thanksgiving Day at age forty-nine. I was playing touch football with my family in the backyard where I was tackled by a mild heart attack. Thank you, Rachelle, and to our daughter, Reyna, for the lifesaving aspirin dose. Off we went to the Howard County Hospital emergency room. After being transferred to Johns Hopkins in Baltimore, a total of four heart artery blockages were bypassed. The grafts are still holding up well without any lasting complications. Thank you, world-renowned Dr. Levi Watkins of Johns Hopkins Hospital for a brilliant bypass operation. Thank you, Dr. Groman, for your continued vigilance. I do so much enjoy visiting every six months.

The complete picture of that time frame needs to also include simultaneously having my successful business career came to a full stop at age forty-nine while dealing with this "heart thorn." Our company buyout was being negotiated and management decided that I was not to be offered a new position in the newly restructured company. According to our restricted stock purchase agreement, I was made a fair offer for my company shares. The offer amounted to the equivalent of fifteen years of compensation at my current salary in cash. It was a lump sum payment equivalent to fifteen years advance compensation for work. Sort of an early retirement package.

In exchange for my shares, a non-compete clause precluded me from performing any work in my field for a five-year period. Also, there was a nondisclosure clause restricting any and all discussion of the buyout terms with anyone in my industry. Violation could result in a forfeiture of the entire lump sum payment. It seemed that complete isolation from lifelong industry friendships was intended. Even a casual conversation had the possibility to explode into news that could place the settlement in jeopardy.

Also, what company outside my industry would want to hire an senior executive and board member, unfamiliar with their business practices, who just had a heart attack? It became shockingly apparent to me that my lifelong career in a terrific industry was over. A tough challenge with four children needing to get through college. Thank you, brother Richard, for the much needed job offer in the golf industry. My family came through for me.

No career, no executive power, no finishing the race—a fading away of career relationships. But with the full stop career end came enough financial resources to carry my needs for the rest of my life. A fair trade-off that had to be accepted.

It was readily apparent that I was being humbled while being set free to pursue a new path in life—one of service in a new way—and so I did! I would have to begin building a new way. On the Rock, my Jesus.

I had been studying the scriptures for several years, wanting to gain firsthand knowledge of the Lord Almighty and his kingdom. Christians encounter a wide, conflicting variety of viewpoints and opinions; when one is guided only by another's testimony, it becomes a challenge to build a complete understanding of the Word of the Lord Almighty and his kingdom. You have to also diligently study and meditate on his Word. The Lord Almighty wants a direct *line to you*. I'm also thankful for the Counselor, the Holy Spirit, for offering his guidance. We are given both a sender and a helpful receiver of his Word. That way, we get the faith and witness that he intends; one-on-one conversations like Job experienced.

I mostly studied alone, researched many online sources, joined a church for fellowship, then found Jesus's embrace! I sought him with all my heart and mind. We both rejoiced in a renewed relationship!

It was after I had first established a relationship with Jesus that I was led to and called into service of the Lord at a newly built church, Ellicott City Assembly of God. I have since served in his church in many various capacities. Over a twenty-five-year span, I have served as an usher, trustee, deacon, adult Bible study teacher, auditor, and now a treasurer for Ellicott City Maryland Assembly of God, soon to be renamed Hope Assembly of God.

CHAPTER 4

THE FULL STOP

One Too Many Thorns in My Crown

For over fifty-five uninterrupted years, I have enjoyed playing the great game of golf! Golf has been a continuous thread uniting my early teenage days with my adult life. I have enjoyed playing golf longer than any other activity that I can remember. Longer than a thirty-eight-year-old business career or my thirty-eight-year-old marriage.

My list of golf trophies seems endless, charity tournaments still abound, and there was that hole-in-one moment after over 5,000 rounds. Better yet, playing the game of golf has taken me all across this great nation and halfway around the world.

There is nothing comparable to playing a world-renowned championship golf course with lifelong friends, industry associates, church members, brothers, family, my sons, daughters, or grandchildren!

I know of no other sport that affords a passionate amateur player the opportunity to walk the exact same venue upon which the greatest professional golf athletes compete. An amateur golfer can play the 2019 PGA Championship venue of Bethpage State Park Black Course and 2019 US Open venue of The Links at Pebble Beach.

An amateur can directly compare his on course performance with the very best of all time PGA Tour Professionals who have ever played the very same course! What great fun!

This year, in 2019, anyone can play the 2020 Ryder Cup course of Whistling Straits in Kohler, Wisconsin. There's no problem getting twenty friends, your sons, and local club members to commit to that challenge! Each amateur in our group will have the opportunity to play every hole that the Ryder Cup competitors will be playing in 2020. On top of that, The American Club staff will treat us like honored guests. Need your shoes shined? It doesn't get any better than that!

My passion for golf grew up as a side benefit of being a caddy at the local country club on the outskirts of Chicago, Illinois. At age fourteen—with a juvenile worker permit in hand and with my slightly older brother, Richard, as guide—I started my first real job as a caddy at Park Ridge Country Club in Park Ridge, Illinois.

The best caddy perk was permission to play a free round every Monday when the course was closed to the members. This began our self-taught first tee program! Talk about the classic movie *Caddyshack*,[2] we lived it out at Park Ridge CC in real life! That was us! *It also turned out that others* in Park Ridge, Illinois at that time were busy planning on becoming president of the USA. We always thought that we had made a wise choice knowing our limits!

My brother swears that Bill Murray caddied a few times with us at Park Ridge Country Club for special club competitions and

---

[2] Ramis, Harold, dir. *Caddyshack*. 1980; Los Angeles, CA: Orion Pictures, 1980.

member-guest tournaments. We also played quite a few of the Park District Golf courses in the Chicagoland area.

As a beginning B-rated caddy, the eighteen-hole pay rate started at $1.75 a bag plus a $0.50 tip for a four-and-a-half-hour loop. Impressive!

We quickly learned that golf is a gentleman's game whereupon one shows courtesy to his fellow players and opponents. Opponents always donned and shook hands on the eighteenth green after the match.

When on the course, you learned to say "Nice shot!" to everyone, your "loop", his playing partner, and especially your "loop" opponents! Golf relationships developed into a respect for the other fellow's best playing effort. Handicaps tend to even out various skill levels for fairer score keeping. It's a game where integrity and perseverance means a great deal. Golf is a life-building experience. The First Tee commercials all show that!

I eventually was made an honor caddy and caddied for NFL Hall of Famer, Bart Star; College Hall of Famer, Paul Christman; and World Golf Hall of Famer, Chick Evans. Bill Loeffler was our caddy master—always with the toothpick. Hey, we got close to famous hero type folks!

As years passed, I eventually became a single digit handicapper who was invited to play in numerous competitions. But better than all, golf travel gave me the great pleasure of inviting close friends along with my two sons, Ross and Ryan, to experience the finest golf courses that the world offers. Thank you too, travel golf buddies Mace, Ken, Tim, Frank, and younger brother Randy!

Some fifty-five years after being a B-rated caddy, I was privileged to play some of the world's finest courses. Please let me share a partial list of my top golf course travel venues. There have been many more! The point of this short listing is to show that I have been tremendously blessed to play many renowned venues. Playing the best of the best has given me some sense of accomplishment. Yes, let's do play Whistling Straits in 2019!

Here are some of the venues played.

United States

Arizona

We-Ko-Pa, Grayhawk, Troon North, Lookout Mountain, The Phoenician

California

Pebble Beach Links and Resort (Played 2018), Monterey Peninsula CC, Harding Park, Rancho Mirage, PGA West Stadium, Torrey Pines, Rancho Santa Fe, Spyglass, Poppy Hills

Colorado

The Broadmoor

Florida

Trump National Doral, Biltmore, TPC Prestancia, TPC Sawgrass, Innisbrook

Georgia

Sea Island, Masters Patron (2019)

Hawaii

Kapalua Resort, Wailea, Makena Golf and Beach Club, Princeville, Poipu Bay, Wailea, Mauna Kea

Kansas

Prairie Dunes, Milburn Country Club

North Carolina

Pinehurst 2, 4, 7, 8, 9; Mid Pines; Pine Needles; Tobacco Road; Tot Hill; Grove Park; Reems Creek

New Jersey

Metedeconk National GC

New York

Bethpage State Park Black

Nevada

Wolf Creek, Reflection Bay, Lake Las Vegas

Maine

Kebo Valley

Maryland

Waverly Woods (Hole in One), Chevy Chase CC, TPC Avenal, Lighthouse Sound, Whiskey Creek, Bulle Rock

Mississippi

Grand Bear Golf Course, Mississippi National, The Oaks, Dancing Rabbit

Missouri

Saint Louis Country Club, Old Warson, Wolf Hollow,

Bellerive Country Club, Boone Valley, Buffalo Ridge Springs, Branson Hills

Pennsylvania

Marion Country Club, Lebanon Country Club,

South Carolina

Kiawah, Harbour Town, Wild Dunes, TPC Myrtle Beach, Tidewater, Barefoot Resort, Dunes, Oyster Bay, Panther's Run

Wisconsin

Whistling Straits (Planned Fall 2019)

West Virginia

The Greenbrier, Pete Dye Course

Virginia

The Homestead, Primland, Virginia CC, Wintergreen, Golden Horseshoe, Stonehedge, Kingsmill

Vermont

Jay Peak, Middlebury, CC of Vermont

International

Scotland

Prestwick, Turnberry, Old Course, Kingsbarns, Carnoustie, New Course

Ireland

Old Head, European Club, Ballybunion, Waterville, Tralee

When playing Pebble Beach in spring of 2018, it was the first real moment that my amateur golf career was in jeopardy. Painful for my knees and for my hips. I wasn't quite certain what was occurring, just old age was my guess. Later that same year, while playing Bethpage Black during the summer, I failed to finish the round due to excessive pain. Disqualified!

Bethpage State Park Black is a monster to walk. No riding carts are ever permitted. If you watched the 2019 PGA for the championship, you know that Bethpage is very challenging track.

Still, in late summer of 2018, totally unaware that there wasn't any soft cartilage tissue remaining in both knees, for our thirty-eight-year anniversary, Chelle and I flew to Europe for a once-in-a-lifetime Blue Danube river cruise. We explored our ancestry only to be asked on numerous tours whether I needed a wheelchair. Tour guides, shipboard employees, airline attendants were beginning to make me aware of just how incapacitated I had become. This pain wasn't just because I was playing golf.

Just a slow learner who's also in denial, my first priority was to see an orthopedic doctor after our return home.

Reflecting now, over many years, it became clear that my mobility had been continually deteriorating little by little. I was just making do as best as possible and ignoring the pain. I was oblivious that the Lord had allowed Satan to place a "thorn" called osteoarthritis in both knees. Total knee replacement surgery for both knees was the only path forward.

But wait! Let's play just one final round before a full stop! This spring, after many years, my son, Ryan, finally won the lottery for four patrons to attend the 2019 Masters in Augusta, Georgia for the Wednesday practice round.

Walking down to Amen Corner at the Masters was one memorable fantasy, but walking back was just pure torture! But it was worth it! We got to share in the greatest comeback victory ever in perhaps all of sports. Tiger Woods won in 2019 after an inspiring effort to recover from numerous leg and back injuries. It was a Presidential Medal of Freedom effort! Thank you for inspiration, Tiger Woods!

Playing just one more golf round was in the cards on the drive home up the stunning Virginia Shenandoah Valley. Primland was indeed worth it! I played it once on the first day and only rode in the cart on the second day. A true mountain top beauty!

A full stop was finally made after fifty-five years of playing golf around the world! Sadly, it had become too physically demanding even to ride in a cart and play eighteen holes. The last was to just ride in the cart and not play.

Was I to bid farewell to the hope of ever playing the walking only Bandon Dunes in Oregon? Would mountain top Primland in the Meadows of Dan, Virginia be my final travel round?

My pop was right when he said, "Be aware of your environment!" Again, like Paul, a valuable lesson was learned about the sovereignty of our Lord's will. His strength is indeed perfected in our weakness. Our bodies eventually fail, but his strength will raise us up on the last day.

As for me, I now needed his guidance about how to manage my knees of "thorns." These also must be managed like the previous diabetes "thorn" and the heart "thorn," so that I might continue to enjoy life and serve others with the fullest blessings of the Lord God Almighty.

CHAPTER 5

KADIMA

Keep Moving Forward

Pursuit of a diagnosis for both knees and hips began less than a month after returning home from Europe. Initially, my search started with a doctor whose orthopedic practice was orientated toward sports injuries and noninvasive treatments. After looking at both knee X-rays, it was immediately apparent that osteoarthritis had destroyed the medial cartilage—as they say, "bone on bone." Both right and left femurs were now misaligned maybe by as much as fifteen degrees. This was the cause of the hip pain. I could maybe walk one hundred yards. I began a physical therapy program for four months to strengthen both legs for surgery.

My search for a top-rated orthopedic surgeon concluded with Bethesda Orthopedic's Dr. Christopher Cannova, one of the most experienced orthopedic surgeons in the Washington, D.C. area. Dr. Cannova is highly competent at performing total knee replacement surgery and specializes in using patient-specific implants manufactured by Conformis located in Massachusetts. Conformis knees are built to replicate the functionality of the original knee. According to the testimony of surgeons, they manufacture the most improved total knee replacement product in twenty years. This knee implant might even lower my handicap!

Dr. Cannova performs surgery at Suburban Hospital, a Johns Hopkins facility in Chevy Chase, Maryland. Suburban is the winner of the 2019 ANCC Magnet Recognition. Magnet Recognition® from the American Nurses Credentialing Center (ANCC) is the most prestigious distinction a hospital can receive for nursing excellence and high-quality patient care. Only 8% of US hospitals earn the Magnet designation.

After selecting the finest surgical team possible, I was admitted for surgery on April 17, 2019 and was discharged on April 18. Unfortunately, the recovery did not go as expected. Somehow, an MSSA staph infection had set in. Diabetics are typically more prone to acquiring these types of complications. Dr. Cannova had to preform "revision and poly surgery" to wash out the infected implant components. It wasn't until July 12, 2019 that the antibiotic Cefazolin infusions taken through a PICC line were completed. A challenge that the medical team met with the greatest diligence.

Other doctor assisted in the monitoring of my progress in fighting the infectious bacteria. Thank you Dr. Vasilios Prygos, Dr. Rebecca Shaffer; the Suburban nursing and hospital staff; and the Kindred at Home care nurse, Retired Air Force Lieutenant Colonel Taunya Pierce, and physical therapist, Diana Mathews.

Overall, there were eighty-four days of a persistently swollen leg, some twenty pounds of weight loss, days of pain management, sleepless nights, and numerous church prayer warriors. Thank you, prayer warrior daughter, Sherra. The Lord is good! Whistling Straits is in my site!

This testimonial began to be written down during the difficult days of recovery. The story is intended to provide encouragement and deep insight into the purposes of the Lord Almighty in shaping our lives. It's a story worth telling. Thank all of you!

By the way, "*Kadima*" is a Jewish term that means "keep moving forward." The great healer, Jesus, had arranged for all these folks to help restore my mobility. He is faithful! The thorns' effects were mitigated, and we are left with a spiritual lesson about our need for an everlasting indestructible body. We all await being raised up on the last day. But for now, I will *Take a Bite Out of Jesus* to help me deal with my failing body.

CHAPTER 6

ENCOURAGED BY
THE LORD ALMIGHTY

The Compassion of Jesus

In closing, let's recall the previous words of Jesus from Chapter 2, the passage of John 6:35–70. Jesus promised that those who believe and partake in him would be *"raised up on the last day."* It was difficult for many of his followers to understand the offering of his body in faith in order to sustain us through many trials until the last day comes. Communion with Jesus is identifying with all the conditions of his body. Not only from broken and suffering for the covering of sin, but also his resurrected body raised with power to everlasting life and seated at the right hand of the Father.

From Hebrews 4:14–16:

> "Therefore, since we have a great high priest, who has ascended into heaven, Jesus the Son of God, let us hold firmly to the faith we profess. For we do not have a high

priest who is unable to empathize with our weaknesses, but we have one who has been tempted in every way, just as we are— yet he did not sin. Let us then approach God's throne of grace with confidence, so that we may receive mercy and find grace in our time of need."

Let us be encouraged! When we are sifted, we are being refined like pure gold. All things work for the good of God's good and pleasing will.

From Philippians 4:13:

"I can do. All this through him who gives me strength."

Amen.

CHAPTER 7

POWER MADE PERFECT
IN WEAKNESS

Raised to Eternal Life and Given a Body

We carry around in earthly bodies our weaknesses, but new life is at work in us! One day, our earthly bodies will fail, but on that last day, we will be raised unto eternal life. That is the power of the Lord Almighty being shown. His perfect will to raise up my weak, defeated body and to be given a new everlasting body!

So, what will be some of the characteristics of this new Spirit raised body?

From 1 Corinthians 15:42–49:

"So will it be with the resurrection of the dead. The body that is sown is perishable, it is raised imperishable; it is sown in dishonor, it is raised in glory; it is sown in weakness, it is raised in power; it is sown a natural body, it is raised a spiritual body. If there is a natural body, there is also a spiritual body. So it is written: 'The first man Adam became a living being'; the last Adam, a life-giving spirit. The spiritual man did not come first, but the natural, and after that the spiritual. The first man was of the dust of the earth, the second man is of heaven. As was the earthly man, so are those are of the earth; and as is the heavenly man, so also are those who are of heaven. And just as we have been borne the image of the earthly man, so shall we bear the image of the heavenly man."

I'm really looking forward to the last day! Jesus promised me three times that if I take a bite of him now, he will raise me up to have a glorious body having the heavenly characteristics of his.

In summary, the Lord Almighty wants to spend eternity loving every one of us. He wants to bury the hatchet, so to speak. Forget our past shortcomings. There is only one condition. If we believe in his Son, then all heaven rejoices!

From 2 Corinthians 5:17–19:

"Therefore, if anyone is in Christ, the new creation has come: The old has gone, the new is here! All this is from God, who reconciled us to himself through Christ and gave us the ministry of reconciliation: that God was reconciling the world to himself in Christ, not counting people's sins against them. And, he has committed to us the message of reconciliation."

What encouragement that is to all people! So, we press on with these earthly bodies. Mine will continue to "de-volve" with age. My body has not evolved in forty years. My simple logic is that if life can naturally evolve into a higher being, then life also can "de-volve" into a lower being. My observation is that both directions do exist naturally and spiritually within the boundaries established by the Lord Almighty. But the trend isn't always up. There is down too. Bounded is the word.

The Lord Almighty has allowed me to be sifted. He is refining me to do his will. I trust this story blesses you. If a blessing does come your way, I pray that your faith will exalt the Lord Almighty.

We live in a world where many people deny that the Lord Almighty is sovereign and that he deserves our worship. Some who do not yield to his authority and, in their name alone, seek fairness and power. They seek to convince us all about the just nature of their cause. A free society gets to choose their path forward.

However, my prayer is that, along our path forward, we always look to the Lord Almighty for spiritual strength, guidance, and wisdom. In Acts, the Bible names this "the Way." May we obey him and increase our faith in him.

The Lord Almighty is good and lives forever!

Amen! Hope to see you soon on the course again!

REFERENCES

Kenney, Douglas, Harold Ramis, and Brian Doyle-Murray. *Caddyshack*. Directed by Harold Ramis. Produced by Douglas Kenney. Performed by Chevy Chase, Rodney Dangerfield, Ted Knight, Michael O'Keefe and Bill Murray. Warner Bros., 1980.

Warren, Rick. *The Purpose Driven Life*. Grand Rapids, Michigan: Zondervan, 2002.

ABOUT THE AUTHOR

This is the first book written by Rod Hempel. He grew up in the Midwest and studied engineering at the University of Missouri in Columbia. He retired after a successful private sector business career. He and Rachelle raised four wonderful children. He looks forward to traveling with family and friends, and playing with their wonderful grandchildren. He currently resides in Columbia, Maryland.

CPSIA information can be obtained
at www.ICGtesting.com
Printed in the USA
LVHW090413191219
641014LV00001B/4/P